INSIDE THE FLOWER ROOM

SADDIQ DZUKOGI

AF279437

for Mirah, for choosing to grow old with me

This is a work of fiction. All names, characters, places, and incidents are a product of the author's imagination. Any resemblance to real events or persons, living or dead, is entirely coincidental.

Published by Akashic Books
©2018 Saddiq Dzukogi

ISBN: 978-1-61775-639-9

All rights reserved
Printed in China through Four Colour Print Group, Louisville, Kentucky
First printing

Akashic Books
Brooklyn, New York, USA
Ballydehob, Co. Cork, Ireland
Twitter: @AkashicBooks
Facebook: AkashicBooks
E-mail: info@akashicbooks.com
Website: www.akashicbooks.com

African Poetry Book Fund
Prairie Schooner
University of Nebraska
110 Andrews Hall
Lincoln, Nebraska 68588

TABLE OF CONTENTS

PREFACE
by Matthew Shenoda

In Saddiq Dzukogi's *Inside the Flower Room* we are introduced to an intimate and revealing voice, a voice full of clarity that longs to reconcile a familial past fraught with pain, in order to shape a new future. In often searing, candid, and sometimes angry poems, the complexities of the human body and what it must endure are coupled with the complexities of intergenerational strife, as we see a kind of humility and vulnerability rarely seen in the poetry of many men. What's more, is that Dzukogi's craft often takes slight turns, blurring boundaries in surprising ways, working through age old subjects with a finely tuned and freshly focused nuance. In passages like the one found in his poem "Unseen," we witness the way body and place become reconciled as inextricable; the way longing, trauma, pain, and reflection are found in both person and place:

> I can go on, let my voice duplicate
> every salted wound on your body—
>
> until my stories become your bones—
> go on until my body too becomes your body,
> while each abides its own shadows. Please
>
> be each stretched leaf, five fingered palm, a wet reflection.
> Float with me on this long procession of silence, cigarette smoke
> released from between open lips,
>
> the night's transfiguration, an owl,
> the landscape alive on its back, as if clinging to the place
> it began. I can go on until my mouth dries of songs—

Throughout Dzukogi's poems we are welcomed into these spaces of wonder and question. Perhaps most significant is Dzukogi's resistance to definition or sureness, his unfailing openness. There is a journey in these poems that seeks a sense of understanding; a desire from a young father trying to define fatherhood on his own terms, while struggling with the models he inherited. We see this struggle in poems like "The Last Time My Father Hit Me":

> I remember, because he first slid a name into
> my daughter's ear and said *answer*.
>
> The last time,
> the day after Daughter opened an obverse door
> and said *hello*, searching for my voice, her mother's
>
> covered in silver, in a blade of war,
> in the oppression I have been trying to name.
> …
> I want to cry into a self-acclaimed faultlessness.
> I want to appear before Father's next ire
> and burn like papers in flame. To name my child,
>
> Father says, is the ultimate sin. The sugar I know
> turns to shadows, Father is more of odium
> than salve, claims all the bones in my body
> belong to him,

Here we see an intergenerational masculinity working towards a newly imagined set of possibilities. Possibilities that are also captured in his poems, poems like "Insignia" where he writes:

> Keep yourself like a photograph
> inside my heart, these memories

need no filter into the universe,
a forest of eyes open into the figure.
You can keep our love

in a flower vase hung in the bedroom,
fragrant on curtains,
in our underthings,

the closets will hold the scent of our new body
and out in the world, the rest of our lives,
we'll wear each other as insignia.

And in the end it is that hope, that redefinition of how we live, unearthed from an honest inquiry into the past and a yearning for a new path forward, that makes Dzukogi's poems so revealing and welcoming. The poems found here are a rare and much needed intimacy, a tough rooted plant that will flower well beyond this chapbook and into the lives of each person who reads his work. Saddiq Dzukogi is a poet worthy of attention and engagement on his path towards helping define the new generation of African poets.

COME INSIDE

Pilgrim, sit beside me,
in this uncluttered pail,

I shall serve you
my grief as food

& eyes' salty water
as wine. Be ready

like fingers inside a
hollow pocket;

you'll know the inside
of my body,

the sidewalk
everyone tramps,

a lock that welcomes
many keys. Come, pilgrim,

enter the firehose. Know
sometimes keys

do not listen,
just as these keys, my body,

understands. Blunt
or sharp, the teeth

unfasten me;
a bone-faced clock,

a wax with no candle-
thread to burn.

FLOWER ROOM

I look at her and discover Grandmother
lives inside a fruit, fresh off the tree;

a body maps its own origin,
rifles for a familiar place;

self-portrait of a father
in a little girl's eyes.

I look at my child so I can see
what's not familiar,

the way I see the seed
not growing as expected,

the roots first, then the green
offshoot.

When Daughter enters this world,
the silhouette of every body crams

into my eyes,
shadows in a whitc/black

room only a daughter knows,
a father's soft spot, a flower room,

where she can hide spiraled in darkness.
I imagine hiding inside

my loneliness because it is convenient.
Before she entered, my heart frowned

at everything, pomegranate water,
family doll. Everything

weighed down my heart
like a flower at the far edge of a house.

TIME

Like old silk, her rumpled palms
scrub my back—grass
over a river, a street is where
every orphan lives and picks

a name, and because Grandmother wanted to give me a name,
she gave songs to nights afraid
of her frail voice. Silence

decides what space to trade with shadows,
Grandmother says a crescent is an arc
that grows flesh—turns into a circle
before its eyes dim at things;

a clockface that's seen far too much, cradles every day
until it turns a flower for her,
to place behind her ear.
A storm moves through my bones

while her hair runs its teeth over my skin.
She protects me in her arms
like a truly loved thing,
whispers:

only the wind has a pure voice
and time is a frozen face,
a lake, a night that reflects traits
of silence or silence, silence itself.

UNSEEN

The landscape retracts into the night, a room large
enough to swallow all things endured;
a butterfly flirts with the flame creased into the butt

of a cigarette my father drops on the pavement.
I can go on, let my voice duplicate
every salted wound on your body—

until my stories become your bones—
go on until my body too becomes your body,
while each abides its own shadows. Please

be each stretched leaf, five fingered palm, a wet reflection.
Float with me on this long procession of silence, cigarette smoke
released from between open lips,

the night's transfiguration, an owl,
the landscape alive on its back, as if clinging to the place
it began. I can go on until my mouth dries of songs—

my tongue vinegar, my mouth opens to an olive *O*
as silent as a cemetery; be part water, this part
where the sun's rays can't trace a presence

heavier than water; my father as he enters,
and me waiting all day to be unseen;
my mother's palm ready to absorb my loneliness;

a house lead-footed in loneliness—

no one here can save me.
All of us at the dining room table

eating warm eggs dipped in vinegar
and no one can save me;
voices lost in airless fur, waterless air, you

drifting farther away and nothing left, nothing
but my father's stifling voice.

THE LAST TIME MY FATHER HIT ME

I remember, because he first slid a name into
my daughter's ear and said *answer.*

The last time,
the day after Daughter opened an obverse door
and said *hello*, searching for my voice, her mother's

covered in silver, in a blade of war,
in the oppression I have been trying to name.
I have been trying to tell my mother

about the tyranny of her eyes, but Mother is
eventful with temperaments. She does not listen.

I want to cry into a self-acclaimed faultlessness.
I want to appear before Father's next ire
and burn like papers in flame. To name my child,

Father says, is the ultimate sin. The sugar I know
turns to shadows, Father is more of odium
than salve, claims all the bones in my body
belong to him,

says everything from my gene is his,
says I am slave and he, the eternal master.
My grief is a wound refusing to heal.

I feel my limbs inside my lover's heart. She knows
the song I sing when I am hit.

I want to walk through this fire without
being scalded into silence

like a river searching for dawn.
I want to whisper peace into my daughter's ear.

THE PIGEON

sees Baha's future cleavage; I don't
need to wonder what's on its mind.

She is five months old, everything
still forming, an unfolding leaf at the edge

of a cracked earth where only a pigeon knows
pebble from seed. Lying on my lap, my hand is a world

where I love to wash my child.
The bathtub accommodates the daughter,

her head cuts the foam, the milky shower cream
covers every other body part, the bulbs

of the stain remover are thirst-quenchers for her tender skin. Here
the dirty bath water; a pigeon at the window;

the baby's feet soft in my palm. As a father,
I'm learning to wash my grief by bathing my daughter.

IN THE EYE

She needed another eye
when Father said I wasn't

human enough; a sort of beast
night leaves behind the moon.

She clasped her ears
and ran off into a windy sky.

I never saw myself inside
my father's eyes or heard myself

in his voice.
I am competing with the girl

roving freely, clandestine
in my body. I should have perished

long ago. My grandmother palmed
the silence that visited

when the household grew hollow,
when doormats forgot footprints.

I am struggling for a normal
heartbeat, one the world will listen to.

I have made teddy bears my friends,
a friendship born of loneliness.

In my room windows are shut,
a good metaphor for my body.

I didn't know why she yowled
into my ears when she asked

me into her mind,
lit candles that convinced

me that another language
lives under our tongues.

A WONDERFUL PLACE TO HIDE

Night of ruins, finding God I turned
the quran upside down &
read it as a river
following the equinox—

wondered, if I give it a voice,
what song will it sing?
How Grandmother knew—knew
I wasn't making dua to fuse

broken bones back together—
my tongue, purpled, turned
to everyone who listened—drunk
like me, everything is ungoldly,

secrets sun around cast shadows,
faces that want all light—
the muted voice inside me
seized like a little girl

hiding in a closet.
This manly carcass-colored ersatz.
This hand repeats sun, diminishes
in God's eyes, ingesting words

until there is no appetite.
Crumb by crumb, I am everything
inside a bathroom
washing the earth off my body.

This dark, dubious face—this body
an albatross hiding inside the laughter
of Grandmother's flame scarf,
the flame, a pyre

into night's murky pigments—
fixed fur along a spine,
fills every space
in the quran's wide mouth.

PRAYER

I used to pray a lot growing up,
this baby afraid of what remains,

the heavy dark. Dark
shadow's breath breathing back

from every corner of the room.
The dark things that tease sleep, when

Mother's prayers, whispered
and handwritten offerings I could press to my chest—

the willpower of words soaked in blood
for the round body, the heart

that circulates and becomes invisible in the dark
of nightmares. My mother's prayers

an offering on my tongue, a giant apple—
one night forgotten, I woke halfway, a snake

bite on my leg. I watched Mother wipe blood
off my two-pin piercing.

In the morning, I woke up with no wound, no scar.
Father said it all happened in my head.

Mother prayed, her handwritten prayers
wrinkled beneath my pillow,

their crinkles said, *I will tell and tell*
 it so much until it stops making sense.

And I wonder how God
will understand what falls between her teeth,

what lands puréed on my tongue,
what is still being swallowed.

MY SISTER SINGS IN THE TWILIGHT

I try to love my bones
as sickness eats
the enduring happiness
in my body.

I grope in silence like dusk—
my sister's song swells in a room,
pulls me close to her lips.
I pry through earholes &

grow arid, with the crackling
of a putrefying body,
soaked in a voice that quells.
I claw at her song for calm water,

but the igneous pain in her eyes
still ravages my body;
teeth of the spiteful cells
are drawn to me, the way

I am drawn to a cup of coffee
when I work into the night.
The sky dogs stir,
they're heading for my body.

Take me as miracle
in your night—I'll leave my peel
& bones,
as I go on to answer a flower.

RAINBOW BABY

Today we remember all babies born sleeping,
the ones we've carried but never met
—Rhoda Isaac

On the day I celebrated
my 7th birthday,

she came into this world
with a hymn in her mouth,

and now she lives in a room
where Mother seams her grief

into an embroidery on every
fabric she's touched. The moon

is not a thing that blooms
when you cradle stone to glint,

as if wet, Grandmother said.
Like almond, Mother's body

was meant for a seed.
Grandfather said, do not anticipate

harvest when you seed a stillborn.
Many babies have lived inside her,

they'd kick and punch for months
before turning into figurines.

Mother's sorrow is an insatiable wolf,
gnaws at her heart from the inside.

No place else has a silence as profound
as it is in her mouth.

THE LANGUAGE OF SILENCE

I wake inside
the amniotic
sky a foil
of blue
teaching
my shadow
to talk
to a tree
the language
of silence
and see
how it soaks
in its own
silhouette
and builds flesh
like a face
waiting
to be seen
in a bowl of water
the scale
of what is dark
is seen on
a prism
of what is bright
to speak
a language
spoken in silence
every syllable
must hold
the tongue

INSIGNIA

Keep your body
like a neighboring country
close to mine,

let the river flow into us,
coves of blood, making us one,
pulses woven into each other

like braided hair, the lines of our borders
erase as bodies amalgamate
and become whole in one body.

Keep yourself inside my body.
There'll be no longer the need
to think of me when you feel

your bones mutated into mine,
no longer need for talks over the phone.
When we live inside the same body,

you can deliver
words directly to my soul.
Our body is a home

you'll never step out of.
Keep yourself like a photograph
inside my heart, these memories

need no filter into the universe,

a forest of eyes open into the figure.
You can keep our love

in a flower vase hung in the bedroom,
fragrant on curtains,
in our underthings,

the closets will hold the scent of our new body
and out in the world, the rest of our lives,
we'll wear each other as insignia.

WIDOW'S SMILE

There are many secrets to a widow's smile,
sometimes it is a wall and every little

sadness hangs there like little pictures
of what she has endured.

Once I entered a common room and
it looked like my mother's mind,

the paintings on the walls were
a gallery of all the ones who are lost,

like my father.
Cobwebs on the corners of the window

means no more visitors can come.
I hear the last man who also tried to walk

into Mother's life was as frightened
by her silence as I am of this room.

Her heart is no longer a gallery,
but a warehouse reminiscent of this room—

only memories of what it used to hold,
now occupied by spiders and their circus,

and yet she tries to bend all the lines on her face
in every way to make us think she is smiling.

BLACK EYES

Through the tiny holes in the roof
she glowers at the sky. She's a house,
allows her hollow rooms
to see the rain—Father is the rain—touching
many bodies at a time. He drapes her
in a harsh climate of infidelity, opens her—
door to door—to the last skin, false
hands of the sun. He sears her
like a green fruit, suspends her
from each tree branch. Mother
is a suitcase ready for the road, still the only woman
who searches for starlight in Father's dark
eyes, cloaks the names: Lisa Tania,
Leila Naylah—all the lovers he said
were just friends. Her eyes say
she'll drive a dagger through his belly
if he dares a step towards her.
He falls like a fish into Mother's net,
her eyes enflamed, pink & wine,
she covers them in shades
as if she'd acquired black eyes.
She knows, knows
she's no longer his dream.
He proclaims to a mirror,
*I don't see her as the crowned-
head she was a while ago.* I know the mirror
sees her with a peculiar disgust. I know
the mood she hears & tries
to mold into words, soft—

how her voice sounds
like a voice in a funeral home, brave
to wake up the dead. Outside,
the wind lifts the leaves off the trees Father plants.
They fly like birds, disappear, absorbed
into the air, deliquescent and gone.

FATHER'S DEMISE

The opaque face of things
like stone & water

& my extended family fighting
while the village expects us to soak

in a seawater of mourning.
Father's demise is a dispersing light.

I grumble at the moment
of his passing, my siblings each

trying to hide their happiness,
my shadow is only good at imitating

my posture. Only Grandmother owns
any genuine grief. The moon hangs

by the window, unable to wash off her sadness.
Night won't penetrate her eyes.

My father's brother keeps
his schemes intimate, like a lonely wife

holds a pillow, he holds what is Father's
in the same way a best man

looks at the bride he is secretly in love with.
My mother once told her friend

he had come to her tiptoeing,
wanting to wear my father's shoes,

but later found my mother's body a room too big for his foot.
My mother doesn't know. I broke

her metaphor just the way she breaks kola
for those who have come to mourn;

sad stories stretching the size, the size
of our sitting room, the size of the whole market.

AYLAN REFUSED THE SKIN OF WATER

A boy all by himself,
came to the shore with no boat
after the sea wormed in and
sunk herself in his stomach and
pushed him to the margin

where clay returns to sand,
when it refuses her skin of water.
The world is giving a funeral
in tabloids; only the dead are in dire need
of where to lie because they rot.
The living are left to wonder

in the sea and its extension—
in search of clouds that do not leak.
You went with the city into the sea
knowing it's a killer who doesn't let you rot
on a street blaring in sniper shots.

Home is now the sea swallowing
and vomiting all who have gone into her mouth,

salty with the scenes of bullets,
pulling men and women to kneel
as they gather what remains of their children.

Home is the road being roved
in search of a house that shuts its doors when you arrive.

CHILD IN A WAR

I have been set upon a knoll
like a half-moon. I want to keep
the picture of my face the day

I lost my only child in a war.
I have come to love his dead body
and I am on my own way to a grave.

The scratches on his flesh
didn't seem enough to kill him—
they say to write on water is to

tell a child to recollect his first cry.
When I stood before an elongated mirror
in a bathroom carrying my child

on my shoulder I said, "Can't
you see he is not a ghost?
He is nothing like a ghost."

I do not see my face, my sorrow
blinds the mirror like my body
blinds my ghost.

My burden has made my legs swell.
They no longer fit into any pair of shoes.
I need to think about the bowl of palm wine

that has drowned my whole life.

My shadow stretches itself
away from my body, the darkness

inside me too profound to serve
as a meaningful companion.
I am a father whose heart is filled

with desire of all the good things
about fatherhood.
I cannot hold how days have fallen

behind me, like the curtain when I entered
my dead child's room.

THE IDP CAMP
after Amanda Joy

The IDP camp is a labyrinth of grief, a place not meant for
making sweetened memories. I do not wish to learn more

about my lover's body, a skin full of retentions, of everything
lost, the mothers, the fathers, my sister; every limb

of my lover reminds me of someone cut off;
to understand grief is to see my face,

a dream dissolving into the day I lost my child.
Expecting no response, I kept touching her neck for a pulse.

I learnt something new about loss. Burying a child is a blessing,
a painful one, less absorbing than picking pieces of your dead

in fragments like parts of a car one tries to assemble,
pieces kept for safekeeping.

My heart learns this new grief, the IDP camp,
a place my face unlearns how to smile. Time to time

I stare long into a mirror until my face blurs and I am unable
to recognize myself, my birthmark disappears into a sky

always heavy, grief makes it so heavy. A song I do not like listening to,
a song that lives in a camp full of sad people. Food shortage is always

on the menu, a sapphire's empty stomach and hunger's sharp canines,
reefing its forelegs on malnourished bodies in tents,

disconcerted by caterpillars, strange faces, empty bowls.
I am praying, but distrust the claims of my prayers, and they fade

like ebbing grace, stiffen my tongue.
How it cracks like everything made of clay.

PARDON

I have consumed my last nightmare, lifted from the eye in the grass upon a hill-
side—piles of fathers—children—mothers who will never return to their families,
not even as corpses.   The city I left last night has grown so small it can lie
quietly under a table as debris.

Everything now lives in a field of memoirs. The town square is lying down like a
cub's skeleton   and even the market is sleeping like an elephant whose dead body
has been ravaged by hyenas. Every little song that stood as a hut has been reduced
to harvest ruins.

                    I blame this on the night—oars with Grandmother's voice
running past & continuing on,
only the road to my village has folded up back in time.
The last time I saw Grandmother, the wood was blowing smoke at her face while
        she was trying

to make a fire—her cough was a knife that couldn't cut her persistence.
I took the long walk & bent into the night on her way to my village,
the footpath had folded back in time.

Fences of tree branches were buried, tangled together
like a pile of dead bodies after a great massacre—it was a great massacre.
Once I asked a window for a story & it gave me landscape in the full spectrum of
        chaos.

The night delivers dreaded silence—grief continues to flow,
like a large body of water
watching for families long after they've passed on.

ACKNOWLEDGMENTS

Thanks to the editors of the following publications in which some of these poems first appeared, sometimes in different forms:

African American Review: "Time"
New Orleans Review: "A Wonderful Place to Hide"
Prachya Review: "The Language of Silence"
Verity La: "Come Inside"
Alephi: "Father's Demise"
Welter: "Rainbow Baby"
Trailhead: "Child in a War"
Off the Coast: "Aylan Refused the Skin of Water"
Crab Orchard Review: "Unseen"
Tinderbox Poetry Journal: "Prayer"
Poetry Salzburg Review: "In The Eye," "Insignia," "My Sister Sings in the Twilight," "Widow's Smile"